Seattle STORM

by Luke Hanlon

Copyright © 2026 by Press Room Editions. All rights reserved. No part of this book may be used or reproduced in any manner whatsoever, including internet usage, without written permission from the copyright owner, except in the case of brief quotations embodied in critical articles and reviews.

Book design by Kate Liestman
Cover design by Kate Liestman

Photographs ©: Matt York/AP Images, cover; Julio Aguilar/Getty Images Sport/Getty Images, 4, 7, 8; Elaine Thompson/AP Images, 10, 16; Lisa Blumenfeld/Getty Images Sport/Getty Images, 13; Jeff Vinnick/Getty Images Sport/Getty Images, 14; Christian Petersen/Getty Images Sport/Getty Images, 19; John Froschauer/AP Images, 21; Leon Bennett/Getty Images Sport/Getty Images, 22; Nick Wass/AP Images, 25; Bruce Bennett/Getty Images Sport/Getty Images, 27; Steph Chambers/Getty Images Sport/Getty Images, 29

Press Box Books, an imprint of Press Room Editions.

ISBN
979-8-89469-019-3 (library bound)
979-8-89469-032-2 (paperback)
979-8-89469-057-5 (epub)
979-8-89469-045-2 (hosted ebook)

Library of Congress Control Number: 2025932152

Distributed by North Star Editions, Inc.
2297 Waters Drive
Mendota Heights, MN 55120
www.northstareditions.com

Printed in the United States of America
082025

ABOUT THE AUTHOR

Luke Hanlon is a sportswriter and editor based in Minneapolis. He's written dozens of nonfiction sports books for kids and spends a lot of his free time watching his favorite Minnesota sports teams.

TABLE OF CONTENTS

CHAPTER 1
SELFLESS TEAMMATE   **5**

CHAPTER 2
LIGHTNING STRIKE   **11**

CHAPTER 3
REIGNING CHAMPS   **17**

CHAPTER 4
STORMING BACK   **23**

SUPERSTAR PROFILE
SUE BIRD   **28**

QUICK STATS	30
GLOSSARY	31
TO LEARN MORE	32
INDEX	32

CHAPTER 1

SELFLESS TEAMMATE

Sue Bird dribbled around a screen. She stopped just in front of the three-point line. Bird quickly dished the ball to Jewell Loyd. The Seattle Storm guard was wide open for a three-pointer. Her shot hit nothing but net.

Loyd's bucket gave the Storm their first points of the game. They were

Sue Bird averaged 9.2 assists per game during the 2020 playoffs.

facing the Las Vegas Aces in Game 1 of the 2020 Women's National Basketball Association (WNBA) Finals. The Aces had jumped out to an 8–0 lead. Bird's assist to Loyd sparked Seattle's offense. And it served as a sign of things to come.

Later in the first quarter, the Storm forced a Las Vegas turnover. Bird received the ball well behind the half-court line. She saw Storm forward Breanna Stewart streaking down the floor. So, Bird lofted a perfect pass into Stewart's stride. Stewart buried a layup to give the Storm their first lead of the game.

Bird was one of the best passers the league had ever seen. She rarely looked to shoot against the Aces. Instead, she

Jewell Loyd (left) averaged 18.3 points per game during the 2020 Finals.

kept setting up her teammates to score. Passing to Loyd and Stewart helped. By halftime, Bird had 10 assists. Meanwhile, Loyd and Stewart combined to score

Breanna Stewart takes a shot during Game 1 of the 2020 Finals.

35 points. They helped Seattle lead by 17 at the break.

The Aces battled back. By the start of the fourth quarter, the Storm led by only two. Stewart helped build on the

Seattle lead, though. She opened the fourth quarter with 11 straight points. Bird assisted two of her buckets.

The Storm led 85–72 midway through the fourth quarter. Bird ran Seattle's offense again. She passed to Stewart to set up an easy basket. Bird now had 16 assists. That shattered the record for most assists in a WNBA Finals game. More importantly, her passing helped the Storm beat the Aces 93–80.

PASSING AN ICON

Sue Bird played in 60 playoff games in her career. She recorded 364 assists in those games. When she retired, no player had more playoff assists. However, New York Liberty guard Courtney Vandersloot broke Bird's record in 2024. And she did it by setting up Breanna Stewart to score.

CHAPTER 2

LIGHTNING STRIKE

Before the 2000 season, the WNBA added four new teams. The Seattle Storm were one of them. The Storm built their roster through an expansion draft. However, the team didn't have many talented players. So, they struggled to win games. The Storm finished the 2000 season with a 6–26 record. That was the worst record in the league.

Lauren Jackson averaged 15.2 points per game in 2001.

Those losses came with one benefit. The Storm received the top pick in the 2001 draft. They used it on Lauren Jackson. The forward was from Australia. At the 2000 Olympics, Jackson had led her country to a silver medal. Scouts believed her skills would lead to success in the WNBA.

Jackson proved those scouts right. The 6-foot-6 (198-cm) forward could score against anyone. And she grabbed loads of rebounds. Jackson made the All-Star Game as a rookie. However, the Storm still didn't win many games.

Seattle had the top pick again in 2002. This time, the Storm drafted Sue Bird. The point guard had great vision. Bird clicked

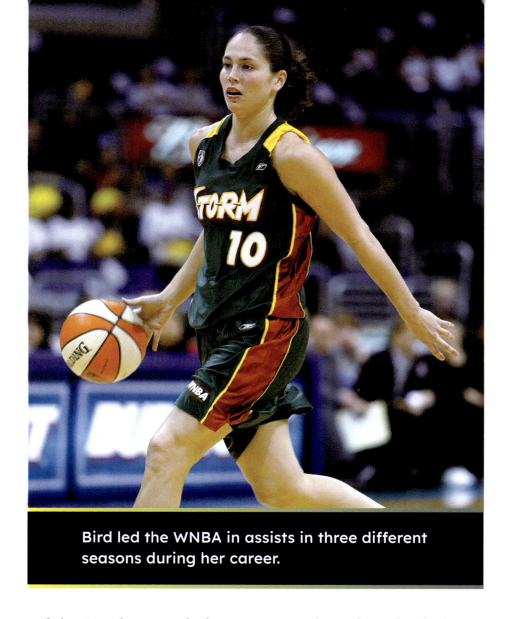

Bird led the WNBA in assists in three different seasons during her career.

with Jackson right away. The duo led the Storm to the playoffs for the first time. But the Los Angeles Sparks swept them in the first round.

Betty Lennox averaged 14.6 points per game during the 2004 playoffs.

Bird and Jackson helped Seattle's offense thrive. Then the team added Betty Lennox before the 2004 season. The veteran guard provided more scoring.

The Storm made it back to the playoffs in 2004. This time, they beat the Minnesota Lynx in the first round. The Storm lost Game 1 in the next round to the Sacramento Monarchs. Another loss would end Seattle's season. But over the next two games, Jackson scored 50 points. The Storm won both games, earning a trip to the WNBA Finals.

Seattle opened the Finals with a close loss to the Connecticut Sun. After that, Lennox took over the series. She led Seattle in scoring the next two games. Her heroics helped the Storm rally to win their first WNBA title.

HISTORIC COACH

Anne Donovan became Seattle's head coach in 2003. A year later, she helped the Storm win their first title. Donovan became the first woman to coach a team to the WNBA title. At 42 years old, she was also the youngest WNBA coach to win a championship.

CHAPTER 3

REIGNING CHAMPS

Seattle didn't slow down after winning the 2004 title. Lauren Jackson remained one of the league's top scorers. And Sue Bird continued to rack up assists. The Storm returned to the playoffs in 2005. They traveled to Houston and beat the Comets in Game 1 of the first round. But the Comets bounced back. They won the

Jackson averaged 7.7 rebounds per game during her WNBA career.

next two games in Seattle to end the Storm's season.

That loss started a trend for Seattle. For the next two years, the Storm lost in the first round of the playoffs. After the 2007 season, Anne Donovan stepped down as coach. Seattle replaced her with Brian Agler.

The Storm traded away their first-round pick in 2008. In return, they got Swin Cash. The forward had won two

ALL-AROUND STAR

Lauren Jackson did it all in 2007. She led the league in scoring with 23.8 points per game. She also grabbed the most rebounds in the league. Those stats helped Jackson win the league's Most Valuable Player (MVP) Award. Jackson also stacked up blocks that season. She earned Defensive Player of the Year honors as well.

Swin Cash played in the All-Star Game twice with the Storm.

championships with the Detroit Shock. The Storm hoped Cash's experience would lift them to another title.

19

The new pieces proved to be a great fit. Seattle posted a 22–12 record in the 2008 regular season. The team had never won that many games before. But the playoffs remained a problem. The Los Angeles Sparks beat the Storm in the first round. A year later, the Sparks knocked out Seattle again.

The early exits didn't keep the Storm down. In 2010, they had the best record in the league. The Storm opened the playoffs with four straight wins to head back to the Finals.

Game 1 came down to the wire. The Storm were tied 77–77 with the Atlanta Dream. Bird had the ball with less than eight seconds left. She dribbled around

Bird takes a shot late in Game 1 of the 2010 Finals.

a screen. Then she pulled up for a jumper. Her shot fell through with 2.6 seconds left. Seattle held on to win the game.

The Dream kept the next two games close, too. But the Storm won both and swept the series. After five straight early exits, the Storm were champions again.

CHAPTER 4

STORMING BACK

The Storm traded away Swin Cash after the 2011 season. Then Lauren Jackson retired from the WNBA in 2012. In 2014, Seattle missed the playoffs for the first time in 11 years. But the Storm quickly rebuilt through the draft.

Seattle had the top pick in 2015. The team drafted guard Jewell Loyd.

Breanna Stewart (left) averaged 18.3 points and 9.3 rebounds per game as a rookie in 2016.

A year later, the Storm had the top pick again. They selected forward Breanna Stewart. Both players provided instant scoring for Seattle. By 2016, the Storm were back in the playoffs.

Seattle lost in the first round in both 2016 and 2017. However, the Storm were ready to make a run in 2018. They faced the Phoenix Mercury in the semifinals. In Game 1, Loyd drained a late bucket to seal the win. Then Sue Bird's

INSTANT SUCCESS

It didn't take long for the Storm's top picks to adjust to the WNBA. Jewell Loyd won the league's Rookie of the Year Award in 2015. Breanna Stewart won the award in 2016. They became the first teammates to win the award two years in a row.

Bird holds the WNBA Championship Trophy after the Storm won the 2018 Finals.

clutch scoring lifted Seattle to a win in Game 2. Stewart closed out the series. She scored 28 points in Game 5 to send Seattle back to the Finals.

Stewart continued her hot streak in the Finals. She averaged 25.7 points per game against the Washington Mystics. The Storm secured their third WNBA title with a sweep.

Bird missed the 2019 season due to an injury. So did Stewart. With their two stars back in 2020, the Storm dominated. They lost only four games in the regular season. Then they swept the Minnesota Lynx in the semifinals to return to the Finals.

The Las Vegas Aces had the same regular-season record as the Storm. But they were no match for Bird, Loyd, and Stewart. The Storm swept the series. They became just the third WNBA team to win four championships.

Seattle remained a contender through 2022. However, Bird retired after that season. And Stewart left in free agency. As a result, the Storm struggled in 2023.

Nneka Ogwumike (3) made 51 percent of her shots in 2024.

But they signed Nneka Ogwumike before the 2024 season. The All-Star forward helped Seattle return to the playoffs. Storm fans hoped Ogwumike could win them a fifth title.

SUPERSTAR PROFILE

SUE BIRD

No player has meant more to the Seattle Storm than Sue Bird. The Storm had never made the playoffs when they drafted her in 2002. Over the course of 19 seasons, Bird helped the team make four trips to the Finals. And the Storm won all four times.

Many great point guards have played in the WNBA. None have enjoyed as much success as Bird. Her great passing skills allowed her to rack up assists. In 2017, Bird became the WNBA's all-time assist leader. She retired with 3,234 assists. Those stats helped Bird make a record 13 All-Star teams.

Bird often passed to her teammates. But she also made plenty of big shots when Seattle needed them. Whatever helped the team win, Bird would do it. She finished her career with 336 wins. When she retired, no player had won more WNBA games than Bird.

In 2021, the WNBA named Bird one of the 25 greatest players in league history.

QUICK STATS

SEATTLE STORM

Founded: 2000

Championships: 4 (2004, 2010, 2018, 2020)

Key coaches:
- Anne Donovan (2003-07): 93-77, 8-8 playoffs, 1 WNBA title
- Brian Agler (2008-14): 136-102, 11-10 playoffs, 1 WNBA title
- Dan Hughes (2018-19, 2021): 49-25, 7-3 playoffs, 1 WNBA title

Most career points: Sue Bird (6,803)

Most career assists: Sue Bird (3,234)

Most career rebounds: Lauren Jackson (2,444)

Most career blocks: Lauren Jackson (586)

Most career steals: Sue Bird (724)

Stats are accurate through the 2024 season.

GLOSSARY

clutch
Having to do with a difficult situation when the outcome of the game is in question.

draft
An event that allows teams to choose new players coming into the league.

expansion draft
A special draft that allows a new team to select players from existing teams.

roster
A list of players on a team.

scouts
People who look for talented young players.

screen
When an offensive player blocks a defender to create space for a teammate.

swept
Won all the games in a series.

veteran
A player who has spent several years in a league.

vision
The ability to see how a play is developing and to know what will happen next.

TO LEARN MORE

Mattern, Joanne. *Sue Bird*. Focus Readers, 2022.

O'Neal, Ciara. *The WNBA Finals*. Apex Editions, 2023.

Whiting, Jim. *The Story of the Seattle Storm*. Creative Education, 2024.

MORE INFORMATION

To learn more about the Seattle Storm go to **pressboxbooks.com/AllAccess**. These links are routinely monitored and updated to provide the most current information available.

INDEX

Agler, Brian, 18
Atlanta Dream, 20–21

Bird, Sue, 5–9, 12, 14, 17, 20–21, 24–26, 28

Cash, Swin, 18–19, 23
Connecticut Sun, 15

Donovan, Anne, 15, 18

Houston Comets, 17

Jackson, Lauren, 12–15, 17–18, 23

Las Vegas Aces, 6, 8–9, 26
Lennox, Betty, 14–15
Los Angeles Sparks, 13, 20
Loyd, Jewell, 5–8, 23–24, 26

Minnesota Lynx, 14, 26

New York Liberty, 9

Ogwumike, Nneka, 27

Phoenix Mercury, 24

Sacramento Monarchs, 15
Stewart, Breanna, 6–9, 24–26

Vandersloot, Courtney, 9

Washington Mystics, 25